60

D0550162

Mit‌‌‌ d
educated at Mill Hill School and the LSE, where

1413 / 13

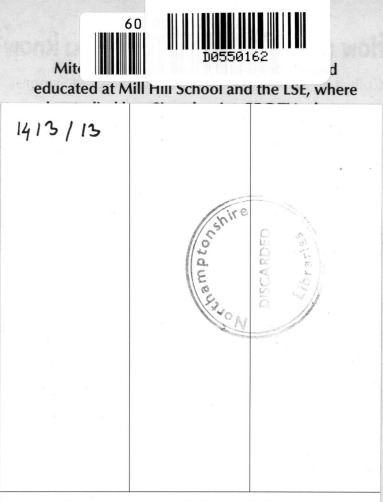

How much yucky stuff do you know?

Collect all these gross facts books by Mitchell Symons!

AVAILABLE NOW!

MITCHELL SYMONS

THAT'S SO GROSS!

ANIMALS

RED FOX

THAT'S SO GROSS! ANIMALS
A RED FOX BOOK 978 1 849 41187 5

Published in Great Britain by Red Fox,
an imprint of Random House Children's Books
A Random House Group Company

This edition published 2011

1 3 5 7 9 10 8 6 4 2

Mixed Sources
Product group from well-managed
forests and other controlled sources
www.fsc.org Cert no. TT-COC-2139
© 1996 Forest Stewardship Council

[The Random House Group Limited supports the Forest Stewardship Council (FSC), the
leading international forest certification organization. All our titles that are printed on
Greenpeace-approved FSC-certified paper carry the FSC logo. Our paper procurement
policy can be found at www.rbooks.co.uk/environment.]

Set in Optima

RANDOM HOUSE CHILDREN'S BOOKS
61–63 Uxbridge Road, London W5 5SA

www.kidsatrandomhouse.co.uk
www.rbooks.co.uk

Addresses for companies within The Random House Group Limited can be found at:
www.randomhouse.co.uk/offices.htm

THE RANDOM HOUSE GROUP Limited Reg. No. 954009
A CIP catalogue record for this book is available from the British Library.

Printed in the UK by CPI Bookmarque, Croydon, CR0 4TD

INTRODUCTION

Welcome to a brand-new series of books, which all have one thing in common: they're all intended to be ENGROSSING – with the emphasis on the third, fourth, fifth, sixth and seventh letters.

I've selected facts that are particularly gruesome in the hope that you will be disgusted and entertained in equal measure. Occasionally – very occasionally – I have used a fact from one of my other books (there's a list overleaf, but my editor and I know them fondly as *BUM, BOGEYS, POO, FARTS, EAR WAX, PUKE* and *LOOS*). I've only done this where it fits in so perfectly that *not* to do it would be even worse!

There are three other books in this series. If you get them all, then you'll know as much as I do – or, indeed, *more* because as soon as I discover a new fascinating fact, I promptly forget at least two old ones! I think my brain's storage section has reached its full capacity.

As usual, I have a lot of 'thank yous'. The most

important people are (in alphabetical order):
Nigel Baines, Lauren Buckland, Penny Chorlton,
Annie Eaton, Charlie Symons, Jack Symons and
Dominica Jonscher.

In addition, I'd also like to thank the following
people for their help, contributions and/or
support: Gilly Adams, Luigi Bonomi, Paul
Donnelley, Jonathan Fingerhut, Jenny Garrison,
Bryn Musson, Mari Roberts, Louise Symons and
Rob Woolley.

As I always write at this point, if I've missed
anyone out, then please know that – as with
any mistakes in the book – it is, as ever, entirely
down to my own stupidity.

Mitchell Symons, 2011

www.mitchellsymons.co.uk

ENGROSSING HUNTERS

The law of the wild is simple but stark. The carnivores (meat eaters) eat the herbivores (plant eaters); the large and fast animals eat the small and slow animals.

The good news – from our point of view – is that despite the huge number of animals that are faster and stronger than us, there are very few instances of animals eating people. And when it does occur, it's usually only because the animal feels threatened.

The hippopotamus – or hippo for short – is a good example of this. Hippos kill more humans than any other mammal, including lions and tigers. The hippo is extremely aggressive, fearless of humans and totally unpredictable: it

can charge without warning – often overturning boats in the river if it feels like it.

But here's the thing: it's a vegetarian – *not* a carnivore – so it only attacks because it doesn't like humans invading its territory. Most human deaths-by-hippo happen when a person gets between the hippo and deep water or between a mother and her baby (calf). In other words, hippos attack in order to defend themselves, their offspring and their territory.

And when they do attack, it's *really* scary. They bellow and make a ground-rumbling charge – swinging their heads like giant sledgehammers, with their massive mouths open to display their huge canine teeth and sharp incisors.

When they catch a person – and they almost always do as they can run at up to 30 miles per hour (and move incredibly fast through the water too) – they kill them with a single bite.

That's it: game over.

By the way, just because you see pictures of hippos yawning or wallowing in mud, don't think that they're lazy or sluggish. The yawn is designed to show off their awesome teeth to any animal foolhardy enough to even consider trying it on. As for the mud baths, they take these to keep cool. Interestingly, their closest animal relative is actually the whale.

Crocodiles are seven-metre-long killing machines. They don't go looking for humans, but they'll kill any that come their way. They'll even take on sharks. They don't swallow people (you'll be glad to know). No, instead, they break us in half or slice us into pieces – making us much easier for other passing creatures to eat.

It almost makes you fond of sharks. Well, *almost* . . . Sharks are prolific killers. They're fast, have sharp teeth and the best sense of smell of all fish. They can detect one part blood in one hundred million parts of water and can even sense the heartbeat of other fish.

Fortunately, they rarely kill people. In any given year, there are very few shark killings – which is why they tend to make the headlines when they do happen. The fact is that sharks are much more likely to eat people who have already drowned than they are to attack living humans.

Probably the worst ever shark attack was in 1945, during the Second World War. A United States warship was torpedoed and sunk in the South Pacific, leaving 1,000 crew members in the water. Before they could be rescued, over 600 of them had been eaten by sharks.

But although shark attacks are rare, it doesn't stop us fearing them, just as people in India fear 'man-eating' tigers. The label 'man-eating' is only given to tigers that have killed three or more people. Ironically, man-eating tigers aren't the strongest tigers, but are simply too old to capture wild animals and so settle for humans instead.

Snakes are often a big worry to any people who share their habitat. Although some species – like the ones found in and around the UK – are totally harmless, there are some really nasty killers in the snake world. The tiger snake's bite causes death in 12 hours – unless anti-venom is taken within 30 minutes of the bite.

The king cobra is the world's largest poisonous snake. Its bite can be fatal for humans and just a single puncture from its venomous fangs can kill an elephant in only four hours.

Coyotes rarely attack people but when they do, it can be lethal. In 2009 a rising Canadian singer/songwriter named Taylor Mitchell, aged just 19, was hiking alone on the Syline Trail in Cape Breton Highlands National Park, Canada, when a pair of coyotes attacked her. Tourists, hearing her screams, rushed to her aid and found her bleeding heavily from multiple wounds all over her body. She died soon after. One of the animals was later shot by the Royal Canadian Mounted Police, but the other got away.

Because of their name, many people assume that killer whales kill people. In fact, that's not how they got their name. They were originally called 'whale killers' by sailors who witnessed them attacking larger species of whale. Over the years, 'whale killers' became known as 'killer whales'. Thankfully, they don't attack people but they do sometimes kill other whales, hunting them in packs. For this reason, they are also known as the 'wolves of the sea'.

The Australian butcherbird impales insects alive on thorns to eat them later.

Kestrels feed on small mammals, such as voles. They identify the areas where voles are living by searching for vole droppings, which reflect ultraviolet light.

About 600 species of plants are carnivorous.

When a stoat is trying to capture a rabbit, it does a strange 'dance of death', which has the effect of hypnotizing the rabbit so that the stoat can pounce and kill it.

When a lion has eaten its fill, it carries its head high. This is a well-known fact in the animal kingdom – so much so that a well-fed lion can walk through a herd of antelope without scaring them. However, if the lion's head is low, the antelope know it's feeding time and scarper.

Frog-eating bats find their prey by homing in on frogs' mating calls. Frogs, not being as stupid as they look, have cottoned on to this, and so they give short mating calls that make them harder to locate. It's a fascinating cat-and-mouse – or, rather, bat-and-frog – game.

Swordfish can heat up their eyeballs to help them see when they go hunting.

The harpy eagle of South America feeds on monkeys.

A vulture will never attack a human or other animal that is moving.

Green herons catch fish by dropping bits of bread and debris on the surface of the water as bait.

The electric eel is the most shocking creature on Earth. Just one zap from a three-metre-long

eel is enough to stun a person. The larger the eel, the bigger the charge, and it can stun its victims from a distance of several metres.

If you've ever wondered why moles make molehills, it's because they're hunting for worms. When they find them, they store them in their underground larders. To stop the worms from escaping, the moles bite them on the back – in effect crippling them so they can't escape.

The killer whale is the fastest sea mammal – reaching speeds of up to 35 miles per hour in pursuit of prey. It's such an effective hunter that it can even kill sharks. It torpedoes a shark from underneath, bursting it by battering its stomach.

Most hunting sharks prefer prey that's weak or helpless because it's easier to catch. That's why sharks are good at smelling blood – it tells them when an animal (or person) is injured. Sharks usually give their prey a fatal bite, then leave it to bleed to death, returning later to feed on the body.

An owl can see a mouse 50 metres away in light no brighter than a candle-flame.

A Dutch wildlife photographer couldn't believe his eyes when he saw a grey heron catch, drown and then eat a rabbit – in a single mouthful. Usually, herons eat mice, frogs and fish so a rabbit was an extraordinary catch. Herons also steal goldfish from garden ponds, which is why people sometimes put nets over them.

Chameleons can reel in food with their sticky tongues from more than two and a half times their body-length away. The chameleon releases its tongue at 26 body-lengths per second – faster than the human eye can see – hitting its prey in about 0.03 seconds.

Bull sharks have been known to pursue their victims on to land.

Snakes swallow whole animals in one go. Some very large snakes have even eaten deer in this way.

Toads only eat prey that moves.

The golden eagle can spot a rabbit from nearly two miles away.

The Komodo dragon – the largest lizard in the world – is a brilliant hunter. Its keen sense of smell can locate a dead or dying animal from up to six miles away. But it's just as well adapted to killing. Using its surprising speed and an ability to keep on biting away at the underside and throats of animals, the Komodo dragon will take on animals up to 10 times its size (like the water buffalo) or even deadlier killers (like the king cobra). Komodo dragons use their strong tails to knock down large pigs and deer. They also work together in groups to attack and kill bigger prey – sometimes working on a single kill for weeks at a time (which is worth it if it results in a big enough meal – typically, the Komodo dragon's own bodyweight).

ENGROSSING HUNTED

Any animal trying to attack a porcupine had better watch out as they're tough little critters! Porcupines defend themselves with thousands of sharp quills that can pierce an enemy's flesh like sharp arrows. However, contrary to what a lot of people used to think, those quills *aren't* actually arrows: that's to say the porcupine can't shoot them out, but they *do* detach pretty easily and so can end up lodged in a would-be predator's body.

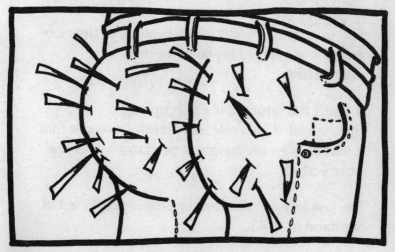

The porcupine's Latin name means 'quill pig' and that's a good description. There are about two dozen porcupine species, and all boast a coat of needle-like quills to give predators a sharp reminder that the porcupine is no happy meal. Some quills, like those of Africa's crested porcupine, are nearly 30 centimetres long. These quills lie flat until a porcupine is threatened, then leap to attention as a persuasive deterrent.

Many animals come away from a porcupine encounter with quills protruding from their own snouts or bodies. Quills have sharp tips and barbs that make them difficult to remove once they are stuck in another animal's skin. The porcupines don't mind, though, as they can grow new quills to replace the ones they've lost.

If that's not enough, if a porcupine is threatened, it also releases an odour so vile that it makes even the toughest predator's eyes and nose water!

The last known wild wolf in Britain was killed in Scotland in 1743.

The female starfish produces two million eggs a year, of which 99 per cent are eaten by other fish.

Hummingbirds are the smallest birds in the world. They're *so* tiny that one of their enemies is actually an insect (the praying mantis).

Hagfish live on the floor of the world's biggest ocean, the Pacific, and they've developed a brilliant technique for repelling would-be predators. Whenever one gets too close, the hagfish oozes slime out of hundreds of pores.

This slime envelops the enemy and eventually suffocates it. However, hagfish have to be careful as they can get caught up in their own slime . . . not a good way to *goo*.

If you're a warthog – I know, it's unlikely but work with me – and you're being chased by a cheetah, your instinct will be to run – very fast and almost certainly faster than any other warthog in the vicinity. However, if you stand your ground, the cheetah will usually leave you alone. I suspect that the key word here is 'usually': you wouldn't want to be the warthog that meets the cheetah that's wise to that trick . . .

Maybe the warthog that stands its ground picked up a tip from the opossum *(Editor's note: Unlikely as they're found on different continents)*. For the opossum is the master of kidology. When an opossum is confronted by a predator, it goes through any animal's standard repertoire of tricks: snarling, spitting, threatening to block it on Facebook. If that doesn't work, the opossum flops onto its side and pretends to be dead. It has to be said that it's pretty convincing. The opossum sticks its tongue out of its mouth and doesn't move a muscle. Then comes the clincher. It releases a truly gross-smelling green slime from its bottom that smells like rotting flesh. Since the opossum's predators won't eat animals that are already dead, they leave it alone and it lives to see another day.

ENGROSSING KILLERS

The reticulated python is the longest snake in the world. Usually, it's about six metres long, but one was found in Indonesia measuring almost *ten* metres. But what concerns us here is not its length, but how it kills the rodents, birds and even pigs that it preys on. It uses its long body to crush the life out of them – a process known as 'constriction'.

The gila monster and the Mexican beaded lizard – both native to the southern states of America and Mexico – look very similar and have something else in common too: they're the only two venomous lizards in the world. They bite their victims, inject their venom and then – and this is the grisly bit – they hold onto their prey for as long as possible to allow the venom to seep into the bite. Then, when it's dead, they eat it.

An eagle can kill a young deer and fly away with it.

Twenty tons of toads are killed on Britain's roads every year.

Lions usually kill large prey, such as zebra, by suffocating them, biting their throats and holding them around the neck with their paws.

Five piranha fish could chew up a horse – *and its rider* **– in just seven minutes.**

It may not be any consolation to its human victims (or, rather, to *their* relatives) but hippos are as tough on other creatures as they are with us. Unbelievably, a hippo can actually snap a crocodile in half. With just *one* bite!

The Siamese archer fish kills insects by squirting water at them from more than a metre away.

Male humpback whales, the largest mammals in the sea, fight to the death as they follow females from the Arctic Ocean to the warm tropical waters of the world, where only the strongest males are chosen by the females to mate.

When it comes to killing, even today's fiercest

beasts could learn a lesson or two from the dinosaurs. The fiercest, most aggressive dinosaur was arguably the *Velociraptor*, but as it only grew to be about two metres long, it would have been no match for the *Tyrannosaurus rex* ('Tyrant Lizard King'), which grew to a staggering 13 metres and weighed 68,000 kilos. The *T. rex* (as it is often known) had huge pointy teeth, which could rip any prey to shreds.

The inland taipan is the world's most poisonous snake – 180 times more venomous than the king cobra. One bite could kill a person within three seconds, also producing enough venom to kill 200,000 mice.

Schools of South American (Pacific) Humboldt squid have been known to strip 225-kilo marlins (large fish) to the bone.

The gaboon viper has the longest fangs and the highest venom yield of any poisonous snake. It's hard to spot as it's camouflaged to blend in with the rainforest where it lives. But if it decides to attack it can move extremely quickly. It sinks its fangs into its prey and injects the venom so deeply that its victims have no chance of survival.

A single toad can eat 10,000 insects in the course of a summer.

The poison-arrow frog has enough poison to kill about 2,200 people.

ENGROSSING FEEDING HABITS

There's a snake that eats the eggs of other creatures. However, it doesn't crack the egg first but eats it whole; once inside its body, its digestive system separates the egg from the shell and then it spits the shell back out.

Frogs and toads never eat with their eyes open because they have to push food down into their stomach with the backs of their eyeballs.

The hippo can last for up to three weeks without eating.

A large whale needs more than two tons of food a day.

A bat colony of five million individuals is capable of eating more than 25,000 kilos of moths in a single night.

A horse eats approximately seven times its own weight in a year.

The South American giant anteater eats more than 30,000 ants a day.

A python can swallow a pig whole.

Insectivorous bats are voracious eaters – devouring as many as 600 insects an hour through the night, every night. Bats can easily eat more than half their weight in an evening. Meanwhile, the fruit bat can eat two kilos of fruit in a single session – so a group of them can easily strip an orchard of all its fruit.

All known amphibians and reptiles that live in the earth below the surface are carnivores, eating creatures such as worms and ants.

Owls swallow mice, rats, birds and insects whole. Then they throw up bits of these creatures and use the puke to feed their young in the nest.

Fish can taste with their fins and tails as well as with their mouths.

A crocodile can't move its jaws from side to side and so it can't chew. Instead, it bites off a lump of food with a snap of its jaws and then swallows it whole.

The duck-billed platypus of Australia can store up to 600 worms in the pouches of its cheeks.

Sharks can swallow anything half their size in a single gulp, but when it comes to eating larger prey they have to do a lot of twisting and turning. Sometimes this leads them to bite their own bodies. You've got to laugh . . .

A leopard can kill an animal three times its weight, but that's nothing: it can then carry its prey up a tree, out of the reach of other animals – especially scavengers, such as hyenas and jackals. After a leopard has had its first meal from the kill on the ground, it drags the animal to the nearest big tree, hauls it up and hangs it over a branch where it's available to the leopard for future meals – a bit like us putting leftovers in the fridge (except that our leftovers don't go off quite so quickly).

Despite its reputation for being finicky, the average domestic cat consumes about 127,750 calories a year, nearly 28 times its own weight in food and the same amount again in liquids.

Using its web – the skin between its arms – an octopus can carry up to a dozen crabs back to its den to eat.

Count Dracula has a lot to answer for. You'd think from its name that the vampire bat would suck the blood from its victims but, in fact, it takes a bite and then licks it up. Vampire bats need two tablespoons of blood a day to survive. It can take 20 minutes for them to get all the blood they need.

It's all very well for lions and tigers and the other big cats to eat their own kills but then there's the problem of all the remains. Fortunately, nature takes care of it by having creatures that simply love eating leftovers – the skankier the better. Vultures, hyenas, jackals and, in more urban areas, crows, magpies and owls, will happily chomp away on decaying flesh and bones. Vultures in particular have stomach acids that are so strong they destroy the bacteria that cause diseases. They spot their next meal using their powerful sense of smell and then swoop – beaks at the ready. If you really want to gross out your friends, tell them that vultures always peck out a creature's eyes before they start feeding on the carcass.

Eating dead creatures can have its disadvantages. Vultures often eat so much that they're too heavy to fly. So they have to throw up to make themselves light enough to take off again.

Baby robins can eat 4.25 metres worth of earthworms in a day.

Komodo dragons tear large chunks of flesh off their prey and swallow them whole while holding the carcass down with their forelegs. However, they can eat a smaller animal – like a goat – whole by using their loosely articulated jaws, flexible skull, and expandable stomach. Understandably, this takes a long time so they sometimes try to speed up the process by ramming the carcass against a tree to force it down their throat. Because of their slow metabolism, large dragons can survive on as few as 12 meals a year.

The giant African cricket likes to snack on human hair.

A snake can eat a whole goat per day. Its gastric juices digest all the bones and teeth – but not the fur or hair, which it has to spit out.

The Argentinian horned toad can swallow a mouse in one gulp.

It can take the Galapagos tortoise up to three weeks to digest a meal.

ENGROSSING FIGHTING

When they get cross, monkeys fling their poo at each other.

When tree snakes fight, they try to swallow one another.

The hyena's jaw is so powerful that it can crush bone in just a single bite.

Eight per cent of dogs will bite somebody before they die. According to statistics, German shepherds bite people more than any other breed of dog.

The heads of a freak two-headed snake will fight over food – despite sharing the same stomach.

The fleshy warts on a male warthog's face protect its eyes from tusk blows when fighting.

The warthog uses its huge tusks for fighting (and impressing) other warthogs. Contrary to what some people think, the tusks are not used for digging for food as the warthog feeds almost exclusively on grass.

Sharks can be dangerous even before they are born. A scientist was bitten by a sand tiger shark embryo while he was examining its pregnant mother. The embryos of tiger sharks fight and even kill each other while in their mother's womb.

Turkeys will peck to death members of the flock that are physically inferior or different.

The cookie-cutter shark is so aggressive that it even attacks nuclear submarines.

Montana mountain goats can butt heads so hard that their horns fall off.

Chimps can be very aggressive with each other – often fighting and sometimes even killing fellow chimps. They also kill monkeys. Do I need to remind you that they are our closest relatives?

Scorpions are solitary creatures. When one meets another they fight to the death, with the winner eating the loser.

ENGROSSING - UNBELIEVABLE

Mike the Headless Chicken – also known as Miracle Mike – was a speckled rooster that lived for 18 months after his head had been cut off. He was thought by many people to be a hoax, but the bird was taken by his owner to the University of Utah in Salt Lake City to establish his authenticity.

This is how Mike came to be the most famous chicken in the world. On 10 September 1945 farmer Lloyd Olsen of Fruita, Colorado, was sent out to the back yard by his wife to kill a chicken so that she could cook it for her mother, who was coming for dinner.

Olsen chose a five-and-a-half-month-old

cockerel named Mike and tried to decapitate him with his axe. He nearly succeeded but the axe missed the jugular vein, leaving one ear and most of the brain stem intact.

Despite this, Mike was still able to balance on a perch and walk clumsily; he even attempted to

preen and crow, although he could do neither. Mr Olsen was impressed by Mike and decided to let him live. He fed Mike a mixture of milk and water via an eyedropper and also gave him small grains of corn. Mike occasionally choked on his own mucus, which the Olsen family would clear using a syringe.

Being semi-headless didn't stop Mike from putting on weight: at the time of his partial beheading he weighed one kilo. By the time he died two years later, he weighed three times that amount.

Mike soon became famous and began a career of touring sideshows in the company of such

THE MIKE FACTOR
AUDITIONS
Be the NEXT
HEADLESS SUPERSTAR

other creatures as a two-headed calf. Mike was on display to the public for an admission fee of 25 cents. At the height of his popularity, Mike earned his owner $4,500 a month and was valued at $10,000. Of course, his success resulted in a wave of copycat chicken beheadings, but no other chicken lived for more than a day or two.

After he died, it was discovered that the axe blade had missed the carotid artery and a clot had prevented Mike from bleeding to death. Although most of his head was severed, most of the brain stem and one ear was left on the body. Since basic functions (breathing, heart-rate, etc.) as well as most of a chicken's reflex actions are controlled by the brain stem, Mike – with the help of the Olsens – was able to remain quite healthy.

During heavy rain, turkeys look up and open their mouths, and some will drown.

Rats multiply so quickly that in 18 months, a single pair of rats could have over a million descendants.

The largest animal ever seen alive was a 35-metre, 170-metric-ton female blue whale.

The largest great white shark ever caught measured over 11 metres and weighed 10,900 kilos. It was found in a herring weir in New Brunswick in 1930.

The largest pig on record was a Poland China hog named Big Bill, which weighed 1,160 kilos.

A 330-kilo mako shark caught off Bimini in the Bahamas contained a 54-kilo swordfish in its stomach – with the bill still intact.

The heaviest dog ever recorded was an Old English mastiff named Zorba, which weighed in at a massive 155 kilos.

The Pacific giant octopus, the largest octopus in the world, grows from the size of a pea to a 70-kilo monster measuring nearly 10 metres across in just two years (which also happens to be its entire lifespan).

The biggest member of the cat family is the male lion, which weighs about 240 kilos.

The world's largest mammal, the blue whale, weighs 50 metric tons at birth. Fully grown, it weighs as much as 150 metric tons.

The world's largest rodent is the capybara. A huge semi-aquatic mammal that only lives in South America and looks like a giant guinea pig, it can weigh more than 45 kilos and grow to more than 1.25 metres long. Its name means 'master of the grasses' and it eats up to 3.6 kilos of grass and aquatic plants every day.

A collie/Staffordshire terrier crossbreed dog swallowed a knife that was only slightly smaller than itself . . . and lived to tell the tale! Kylie, 45 centimetres long, swallowed the 38-centimetre-long bread knife with the sharp end in her stomach and the blunt end sticking out of her mouth! How extraordinary!

A crocodile can't stick its tongue out. This is a means of self-protection. With its sharp teeth and powerful jaws it could easily bite it off!

The lethal lion's mane jellyfish is the largest known species of jellyfish. The biggest specimen ever – found washed up on the shore of Massachusetts Bay in 1870 – had a bell (body) with a diameter of 2.3 metres while its tentacles reached 36.5 metres, making it longer than a blue whale, which is commonly considered to be the largest animal in the world.

A great white shark bit off undersea photographer Henri Bource's leg while he was diving off Australia in 1964. He was soon back at work in the same job, and four years later another shark bit off his artificial leg!

ENGROSSING CANNIBALS

A cannibal is an animal that feeds on other members of its own species. Although human cannibalism is relatively rare and usually practised only in extreme survival circumstances, it's quite common in the animal kingdom. In fact, more than 100 species go in for cannibalism on a regular basis, one way or another.

Let's start with rats. Some creatures are carnivores, others are herbivores, but rats – like us – are omnivorous, meaning they eat pretty much anything: meat, plants, fruit, seeds, insects . . . Unlike us, though, there's almost nothing that they won't eat. This includes dead and dying members of their own species. I know rats have a bad press but you can't help feeling that they do very little to help themselves . . .

Some animals – rabbits, hamsters and, of course, rats – eat their own children. This is NOT done just for the hell of it but is a primitive response to danger. In other words, it's better for mum to eat the babies than for a predator to. Sometimes, it's just confusion: a rabbit will mistake its baby for a mouse or something and destroy it. Sometimes stress can cause a rabbit to eat its young, or it can be a combination of stress and confusion: if the doe eats the babies as she's giving birth, she's probably mistaking them for the afterbirth (placenta), which is an important source of nutrition for all female mammals.

There are other reasons for cannibalism. Perhaps an animal has given birth to an overly large litter and, knowing that she won't be able to feed them all, kills and eats one of them. After all, she's going to need all her strength in the coming days: why should she let good protein go to waste?

Many female rattlesnakes eat their young as a way of recovering lost energy. It's quicker and easier than having to hunt for food, which is a potentially dangerous and time-consuming activity that requires a great deal of energy.

But make no mistake, this isn't just gross: this is

nature in the absolute raw and perhaps gives us an indication of how our most primitive ancestors might have behaved.

With this in mind, you can understand why some species, like snakes, will eat stillborn or deformed babies. It provides more energy/strength for mum and fewer mouths to feed: what you might call a double whammy. In fact, make that a triple: if she kills and eats a diseased baby, she's also protecting the rest of her offspring from catching a disease (either directly from their sibling or, once it's dead, from its decaying carcass).

Generally, though, animals try to avoid eating their own relations – well, it makes it less stressful when the family comes round for tea – but they will still feed on other members of their own species. In some cases, it's simply for survival: animals eat others of their own kind if there really is no alternative – just as we would. In other cases, it's more complicated: for example, large crocodiles feed on smaller crocs, not just for the food but also to keep down the population and so, by limiting the number of crocodiles challenging them for the same prey, preserve their food supply. Ruthless critters, crocodiles.

If cannibalism isn't bad enough, there's also . . . wait for it . . . grossness alert . . . self-cannibalism! Yup, that's right: eating yourself. How crazy is that? But lots of animals do it. The short-tailed cricket is known to eat its own wings and there's evidence of other creatures digesting their own nervous tissue when they make the transition to a new phase of their lives. The North American rat snake, when captured, will try to eat itself – though, in that case, the act of self-consumption might just be an act of suicide. Also, if they get very upset, octopuses can eat themselves.

Mind you, who am I to criticize other creatures for self-cannibalism when I bite my nails? People look at my uneven stubs and say 'You bite your fingernails really badly.' 'On the contrary,' I always reply, 'the disgust on your face suggests that I bite them really well.' Back of the net!

As for bogey-munching, well, I think I have already pleaded guilty on that charge . . .

ENGROSSING ANIMALS ON TRIAL

Nowadays, the thought of animals being tried by courts and, if found guilty, being executed, sounds absolutely mad to us. Sure, we can understand the need to put down a rabid dog or a diseased cow – but we can't get our heads around the whole judicial process being brought to bear upon animals.

But that's not how it used to be.

People used to think that justice had to be extended to animals as well as to people. Sounds fair enough – except they also applied this rule to punishments, and these were as vigorous and as vile as the ones meted out to people.

Animals were sometimes even tortured to make confessions – as if that would work!

The trial and punishment of animals was

especially common in France, and pigs in particular seemed to be the worst offenders. This is probably because during the Middle Ages they were allowed to wander freely around French villages – sometimes with disastrous consequences.

Here are some examples of animal trials from across the world.

1266: In Fontenay-aux-Roses, near Paris, a pig convicted of having eaten a child was publicly burned.

1314: In Moisy, Valois, France, a bull escaped and gored a man to death. When the Count of Valois heard about it, he ordered that the animal be captured and put on trial. The bull was caught, tried and declared guilty. However,

before it could be hanged at the Moisy scaffold, there was an appeal on behalf of the bull. This was considered by parliament, which confirmed the sentence. But how extraordinary that they should have gone to such lengths!

1386: In Falaise, France, a sow (female pig) was accused of killing a baby in its crib. Awaiting trial, the sow was placed in a (human) prison cell. The court heard evidence that the sow had torn the baby's face and arms and decided to apply the Biblical law of 'an eye for an eye'. So they ordered the sow to be mangled and maimed in the head and forelegs (the equivalent to its arms) and then to be hanged. To make the execution as realistic as possible, the sow was dressed in a man's clothes and hanged in the public square as a human being would have been.

1389: In Burgundy, France, a horse was condemned to death by a court after killing a man.

1457: In Savigny, France, a sow killed a five-year-old boy and ate him, with her six piglets joining in. The sow was put on trial, found guilty and condemned to be hanged by her hind legs until dead. But what about the piglets? The court decided that there was a lack of proof that they had helped to kill the child (i.e. that they were their mother's 'accomplices') and, taking into account the fact that they were young and only

following their mother, they were acquitted.

So what happened to them? Did they live happily ever after? Were they feted as local celebrities? Did they sell their wedding photos to *Pigs & Piglets Magazine* (incorporating *Swine Today*)?

Er, no. The court tried to give them back to their owner but told him that he would be responsible for their future behaviour. He didn't fancy the responsibility and so the court gave them to a local noblewoman who, I'm guessing, ate them.

What did you expect? A happy ending? Then you're as crazy as they were!

1510: In Autun, France, the people went to their local bishop and asked him to do something about the rats that were eating the barley crop. Nowadays, of course, we'd simply devise a humane and effective way of killing the rats, but these were different times and the bishop decided to put the rats on trial. He even appointed a lawyer to represent the rats! On the first day of the trial, the lawyer, a Monsieur Chassenee, made the excellent point that it was impossible to distinguish between rats that were eating the barley and rats that weren't. He said that it was therefore necessary for every rat in the area to be summoned to court to plead their case.

So the bishop called on all the local priests to announce the charges in public so that as many

rats as possible would get to hear about it. Yes, I know that this is now definitely entering 'Alice in Wonderland' territory but you have to hold on to the fact that it really happened!

Anyway, despite the local priests making it perfectly clear that every rat was required to go to court to answer the charges, not a single rat showed up. You'd think that this would flummox the defence lawyer, but not a bit of it! He merely pointed out that the rats were, like people, entitled to refuse a court summons if

making the journey to court placed their life in danger. In this specific case, he argued, a rat ran the risk of being eaten by cats, so there was no way they could be expected to turn up unless the prosecution was able to guarantee safe passage.

The trial was adjourned to give the prosecution time to work out how to stop any cat from killing a rat on the day of the trial, but no date was set to restart and so the case was dropped without a verdict.

1692: Two dogs were hanged for witchcraft during the Salem witch-hunt trials in America.

1712: In Brazil, there was a monastery that was plagued with termites. They were eating the walls and threatening the very foundations of the buildings. It was decided to put the termites on trial and they were given their own lawyer (well, they could hardly have chosen their own, could they?). He argued – rather brilliantly – that the termites were entitled to be there and

to do what came naturally to them because they had been there before the monks. After a long legal battle, the court decided that the monks should provide a new home for the termites to live in. According to the trial notes, when the verdict was read out aloud in front of the termites' hill, 'they all came out and marched in columns to the place assigned'. The monk who wrote the notes believed that this was 'conclusive proof that the Almighty endorsed the decision of the court'.

1740: France's last animal trial took place. A cow was found guilty of sorcery and sentenced to death by hanging.

1799: In Woodbridge, England, a judge found two pigs guilty of digging up and eating a corpse. The pigs were sentenced to death by drowning.

1804: In Germany, a horse trampled a boy to death and was taken to court and charged with the crime of murder. The horse was assigned no fewer than three lawyers (it would almost certainly have preferred three carrots) but, after a two-week trial, it was found guilty. The sentence of the court was that it be taken out and shot by firing squad.

1903: Topsy was a tame elephant that worked at the circus in Coney Island in the USA. However, she killed three men (one of whom was a cruel trainer who'd tried to feed her a lighted cigarette). Topsy wasn't actually put on trial but her owners decided that she should be killed. This would be unremarkable but for the fact that they also decided to execute her as a murderer (or, I suppose, murderess).

Having made that decision, they then had to
work out how to carry out this grisly deed.
At first, they thought of hanging her, but the
American Society for the Prevention of Cruelty
to Animals (the equivalent of the UK's RSPCA)
protested and so they settled on electrocution,
a means of execution that had been used on
human murderers since 1890.

So, in front of a crowd of over 1,000 people,
poor old Topsy was fed carrots laced with poison
before more than 6,000 volts were sent through
her body. She was dead in seconds. There was
even a film made of the whole grisly event.

When Coney Island burned down in 1911, the
fire was referred to as 'Topsy's Revenge'.

1924: In Pennsylvania, USA, Pep, a Labrador
retriever, killed a cat belonging to the state's
governor, who immediately ordered a trial. Pep
wasn't allowed a lawyer and the judge was the
governor himself, who sentenced him to life
imprisonment in the state penitentiary (prison).
The story has a happy ending, however. Pep –
now convict C2559 – lived out the rest of his days
being spoiled rotten by every inmate in the jail!

1933: In New York, four dogs that bit a child were put on trial in a court room. Despite the best efforts of their lawyer, they were sentenced to death. However, given that this was 20th-century America and not 16th-century France, they were at least put to death humanely and not executed.

1963: In Libya, 75 carrier pigeons that had carried money for criminals into the country were sentenced to death by the court trying the men. According to the court, the birds were 'too well trained and dangerous to be let loose'. The criminals, on the other hand, were merely fined.

1974: In Libya, a dog was put on trial for biting a person. It was sentenced to a month's imprisonment on a diet of bread and water. After it had served its sentence, it was released.

ENGROSSING NOISE

Cheetahs make a chirping sound – a bit like a bird's chirrup or a dog's yelp, but the sound is so intense, it can be heard a mile away.

Cats miaow to us but they don't miaow to each other.

The low-frequency call of the humpback whale is the loudest noise made by a living creature. It can be heard from – wait for it – over 500 miles away.

The dwarf mongoose has a range of different sounds. If it spots a predator, it screams, meaning that danger is close by. When the threat is further away, it uses a churring sound. When the mongoose finds food, it lets out a shrill twittering to alert its friends. You see, we're NOT the only species that twitters and tweets to friends!

The roar of a male lion, used to intimidate rivals and communicate with other lions, is audible five miles away.

But the noisiest (in terms of the distance from which it can still be heard) land animal is the howler monkey of Central and South America. The sound it makes has been measured at 88 decibels from a distance of five metres, but the little feller can be heard up to 10 miles away!

Why do wolves howl? Is it because they're in pain? Is it because they're hungry? Is it because they've been sent to bed and told they can't watch *The X Factor*? No, none of these. They howl to avoid territorial fights with other packs of wolves. They're saying: 'We're here, and if you know what's good for you, you'll stay clear of us and we'll stay clear of you. By the way, does anyone know who was voted off *The X Factor*? Only we were sent up to bed before…'

Meerkats looking for food keep in touch with each other by making a soft murmuring sound. But when they spot a predator, they cluck and bark to warn the others to rush back to the burrow.

Each species of grasshopper has its own song. This is to stop the different species from breeding with each other. The female needs to know that she's listening to a male from her own species.

On a clear day, a gobbling turkey can be heard a mile away.

Salamanders make squeaking noises when they're disturbed. The Pacific giant sends out a scream and a rattle to ward off enemies. Other salamanders employ an even cleverer tactic – they arch their backs and raise their heads to imitate poisonous snakes.

The noise made by a pistol shrimp is so loud that it can shatter glass.

ENGROSSING ONLYS

Lions are the only truly social species of cat. This means that they live in groups – or prides – with a proper hierarchical (a pecking order that determines which animal is in charge and who does what) structure.

Sharks are the only creatures that never get sick. As far as we know, they are immune to every disease, including cancer.

The starfish is the only creature that can turn its stomach inside out. It is also almost certainly the only creature that would want to turn its stomach inside out. . .

The great white shark is the only sea creature with no natural enemies.

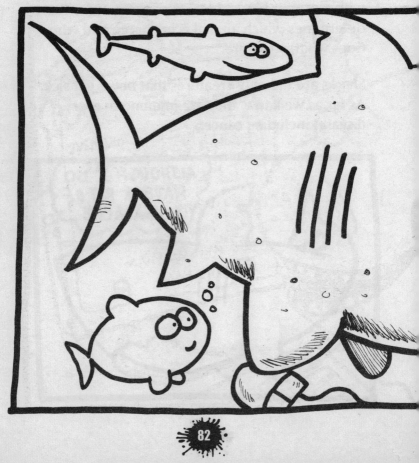

The ostrich, the world's largest living bird, is the only bird that we make leather from.

The Chihuahua is the only breed of dog that's born with an incomplete skull (it has a little hole that closes as it matures).

The armadillo is the only creature – apart from man – who can get leprosy. The armadillo is also the only mammal that can walk underwater.

Mammals are the only creatures that have flaps around their ears.

Many reptiles can replace limbs or tails if they're lost or damaged, but only the newt has the ability to regenerate the lens of its eye.

Pigeons are the only birds that can drink water without having to raise their heads to swallow. Other birds need gravity to help them swallow.

ENGROSSING POO

Cows poo 16 times a day. The average cow produces four times its weight in manure a year.

An elephant produces about 20 kilos of dung a day.

The insides of a shark's intestines are spiral-shaped. This means that sharks' poo is sometimes spiral-shaped.

Poo, turds, spoor and excrement are all different words used to refer to animal faeces. Sometimes, it's more specific than that.

Some poo is named after the individual animal – e.g. cow-pat.

Where poo is dropped in bulk – e.g. by cattle – it's known as dung.

The poo of birds and bats is usually known as droppings.

The poo of any hunted animal – e.g. deer – is known as fewmets (a medieval English hunting term).

The poo of wild carnivores (e.g. meat eaters) is known as scat.

The poo of insects is sometimes known as frass.

Otters' poo is called spraint.

The poo of seabirds or bats is known as guano and it's highly prized as a fertilizer. Indeed the poo of many different creatures is used as fertilizer, or manure – which is why you should always make sure you wash fruit and vegetables before you eat or cook them (do you really need me to spell it out for you...?)

If you've got a pet rabbit you'll have noticed that they eat their own droppings. This is because, unlike sheep and cows which have several stomachs that extract all the goodness from tough plants, they only have one stomach. So they do their digesting in two sessions. First they eat their vegetables and poo little pellets. Then they eat these and digest them again to get out all the nutrition.

Dogs eat rabbits' poo – or at least our golden retriever, Blue, did. In fact, not only did he eat Snowy's pellets, he used to nudge him to provide him with some every time he felt peckish. Bit like a vending machine, I guess!

Dogs also eat cat poo because of its high protein content.

Carnivores' poo is much stronger in smell than that of herbivores.

Animal poo can contain a lot of nutrition. Yup, that sentence was as much fun for me to write as it was for you to read. But, if you think about it (and you will, you *will*), it's important that it does because that's what makes it appealing to other creatures. If they didn't eat it then it would just lie there going to waste. And what would creatures like the dung beetle (the clue's in the name) live on? It's all part of nature: everything in the wild lives in its own ecosystem.

This also helps us to understand the importance of frugivores – that's animals that eat fruit. The frugivore eats fruit, but doesn't fully digest the seeds so that when it poos, it scatters the seeds too – unwittingly helping to plant fruit trees and shrubs. And of course what else is it doing as it disperses these seeds? You guessed it, it's fertilizing them with the very poo that started the process in the first place!

Stand by for something that's genuinely gross . . . elephants eat their mother's poo. That sounds disgusting – well, it is disgusting – but their mums are herbivores and the poo contains essential gut flora. Even so, mums' poo – however much you love your mum and no matter how nutritious the poo might be – should always be off limits.

Vultures poo on their feet to keep cool – especially during the summer. It doesn't do anything to make them smell sweeter, though.

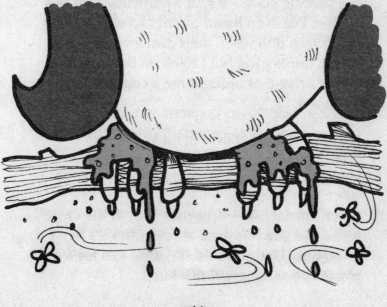

Domestic pets can be trained to poo in a way that suits their owner's convenience. You can get cats and (to an extent) rabbits to use litter trays. From my own experience (as an owner, not as a rabbit), I can tell you that house rabbits trained to pee on newspapers will only pee on newspapers – even when you let them play in the garden.

Dogs can certainly be house-trained not to poo in the house and will wait until they're outside. A really well-trained dog will only poo in a specific place – e.g. in a particular part of a garden. I've even heard of dogs so well-trained that they'll poo when their owners clap their hands. Impressive, but I think on balance I'd prefer a dog that brought me a cup of tea when I clapped.

There's a virus that lives in rat and mouse droppings. Once dried, these droppings turn into dust that can easily be inhaled. Yeughh!

Some animal poo – especially that of the camel, bison and cow – is used as fuel (after it's been dried out). Dung can also be used as a form of plaster (to make mudbrick huts).

I wonder if you can think of any other uses for poo? Here's one you might not have thought of: cow-pat throwing. Yup, that's right. There are contests in which people see how far they can fling a dried cow-pat or a lump of camel dung.

While we're on the subject of poo, I thought I'd remind you about the Asian palm civet, which eats coffee beans and then poos them out partially digested. The result is converted into kopi luwak (civet coffee), the world's costliest coffee.

ENGROSSING INTERESTING

A purring cat doesn't necessarily mean a contented cat. Cats will also purr if they are in pain.

Americans spend 1.5 billion dollars a year on pet food. This is four times the amount spent on baby food. There are more than 100 million dogs and cats in the United States. In total, Americans spend more than 5.4 billion dollars on their pets each year.

The raven tricks its rivals into thinking there's food elsewhere and then sneaks back to eat what it wanted in the first place.

Poison dart frogs lose their poison when they're kept in captivity because the source is a chemical found in small beetles, which only exist in the wild.

Aggressive tigers flash the distinctive white spots on their ears as a warning.

Around the world, there are more than 1,000 endangered animal species.

When black rhinos are fleeing, the calf runs behind the mother, but when white rhinos are in flight, the mother follows the calf.

The bits of an electric eel responsible for its electric powers make up four-fifths of its body. An electric eel produces an average of 400 volts.

Hippos were thought to be able to sweat blood. In fact they excrete a red liquid, which coats their skin to stop it drying out in the hot African sun.

A sheep, a duck and a rooster were the first animals to fly in a hot-air balloon.

Sharks in the seas around Greenland eat

reindeer when they fall through the ice.

Of all known forms of animal life ever to inhabit the Earth, only about 10 per cent exist today.

Female common octopuses (or octopodes or octopi, according to taste) lay up to a 100,000 eggs in a day. They crawl into a dark hole under the sea to do this and nurture the eggs till they hatch. Any idea what happens then?

a They put their feet up and read a magazine.

b They go on holiday to somewhere completely different.

c They die because rearing offspring marks the end of their lifespan.

Give yourself a pat on the back if you chose 'c' because it's the right answer.

The Iditarod Trail Sled Dog Race (usually just called the Iditarod) is an annual sled dog race in Alaska, where mushers and teams of (typically) 16 dogs cover over 1,000 miles in eight to 15 days. Each sled dog burns up an average 10,000 calories a day. This is equivalent to the daily calories required by four grown men!

The poisonous copperhead snake smells like freshly cut cucumbers.

Bison have such bad tempers that they can't be trained.

Whales sometimes rub up against the hulls of passing ships to get rid of parasites on their skin.

Reindeer are plagued by flies that can suck half a litre of blood out of each member of the herd every day. The poor reindeer get so frustrated and fed up with them that they would rather seek higher ground where there is no food, and go hungry, than stay on lower ground where there's more to eat but where the pesky biting flies gorge themselves stupid on their blood.

About 10 times more men than women are attacked by sharks.

There's a Japanese spider crab that has a life expectancy of up to 100 years. Lobsters can also live that long, although their usual lifespan is about 15 years.

Animals are sometimes struck by lightning. They're more likely to be struck than humans because they can't take shelter and because both sets of legs are on the ground, where the electricity is conducted. Horses are particularly susceptible if they're wearing iron shoes. While most humans struck by lightning survive, it's usually fatal for horses – especially if people aren't around to help them with their injuries. Though having said that, death is usually sudden (we know this because horses struck by lightning often have grass in their mouth when they're found).

A male catfish keeps the eggs of his young in his mouth. After they have hatched, if they are in any danger, the father once again opens his huge mouth and lets the youngsters hide inside.

The phrase 'raining cats and dogs' originated in 17th-century England. During heavy downpours

of rain, many cats and dogs unfortunately drowned, and their bodies would be seen floating in the rain torrents that raced through the streets (which didn't, of course, have any drains). This gave rise to the suspicion that it had literally rained 'cats and dogs'.

The turkey was named for what was wrongly thought to be its country of origin. Turkeys actually come from North America, but were imported to central Europe through Turkey, hence the name.

Chimpanzees worm themselves by eating rough leaves to clear the parasitic worms out of their intestines.

Some frogs can be frozen solid then thawed and still be alive.

The mouse is the most common mammal in the United States.

Vampire bats use rivers to navigate as they have such a powerful sense of smell they can scent animal blood even underwater and use it to guide them where they want to go.

Reindeer became extinct in the British Isles in the 10th century. In 1952 they were re-introduced to Scotland.

Sharks sometimes eat fish caught in fishing boats' nets before they can be pulled to the surface.

Most wild birds have a lifespan of just six months.

ENGROSSING - UNUSUAL

One in 5,000 North Atlantic lobsters is born bright blue.

The male seahorse – rather than the female seahorse – carries the eggs, inside a pouch on its stomach.

During the reign of Kublai Khan in the 13th century, the Chinese used lions on hunting expeditions. They trained the big cats to pursue and drag down massive animals – from wild bulls to bears – and to stay with the kill until the hunters arrived.

Wombats roam across an area of up to four hectares around their warren. Unlike most mammals, however, it's the young females who leave the area where they were born, while the males stay put.

Flying frogs change colour at different times of the day and night. During the day, they're greenish-blue then; as twilight falls, they turn green, but when it gets dark, they turn black.

Spotted skunks do handstands before they spray.

In the Caribbean there are oysters that can climb trees.

Because it has no backbone, a 35-kilo octopus can squeeze through a hole the size of a large coin.

The thorny devil, a lizard that is native to Australia, lives in very dry conditions. It drinks by channelling tiny dewdrops that collect on its skin at night along surface grooves to its mouth.

To keep cool, ostriches pee on their legs.

Jellyfish sometimes evaporate if stranded on a beach–they are 98 per cent water.

Sharks have six senses. Besides vision, hearing, touch, taste and smell, they can also sense the tiny amounts of electricity given off by other animals.

Extinct species include: Antillean cave rat, Arabian gazelle, Barbados rice rat, Bavarian pine vole, big-eared hopping mouse, central hare-wallaby, central rock-rat, Corsican shrew, Cuban spider monkey, desert rat-kangaroo, giant deer mouse, Goliath white-toothed shrew, hairy-eared dwarf lemur, Jamaican pallid flower bat, large ghost-faced bat, large sloth lemur, long-tailed hopping mouse, Madagascan pygmy hippopotamus; New Guinea big-eared bat, Queen of Sheba's gazelle, red-tailed black shark, Seychelles giant tortoise, short-horned water buffalo, Tanzania woolly bat, Vietnam warty pig, Western palm squirrel, white-footed rabbit-rat.

ENGROSSING - FILTHY

Although we enjoy a good relationship with many other creatures on the planet, there's no doubt that some of them pose real problems for us. Rats, for example, have given us everything from bubonic plague to Weil's disease, while mice pass on any number of diseases to us (which is why you must never try to stop your parents from calling in the pest controller if mice are found in your home).

We eat shellfish, chicken and pigs but often get food poisoning from them.

But the creature that poses the greatest danger to mankind – right now – is the mosquito. Really? Yes. More people die from malaria – which is of course carried by mosquitoes – than from any other illness associated with creatures.

Some birds use ants to clean them. The birds puff up their feathers and allow the ants to crawl all over them. The ants squirt out an acid, which kills other insects living on the birds, and then eat them. This is what is known as a 'symbiotic' relationship. The birds and the ants both benefit equally but in different ways. The shark has a similar relationship with the wrasse fish. The shark opens its huge mouth to let tiny cleaner wrasse fish nibble lice and dead skin from between its teeth. As the wrasse fish are helping the sharks, they don't get eaten.

Wild yaks secrete a special sticky substance in their sweat which helps to keep their hair matted and acts as extra insulation. This substance is used in traditional Nepalese medicines.

Lions are almost always covered in coagulated blood from their last meal. They have more than their fair share of flies and ticks too.

Sloths have algae growing on them.

As you know, cattle graze on grass, but if the grass is too rich, they get upset stomachs and their poo turns all watery – running down the backs of legs and drying on them. This makes them stink and that attracts the flies. Do feel free to think of that the next time you see a group of cows in a field.

Even pet dogs can be pretty disgusting. Most dogs enjoy rolling in the poo of other dogs – or other creatures, such as foxes. Why do they do this? Because it helps them to disguise their own smell.

Pigs are not – despite their reputation – dirty animals, and yet so many people think they are. Yes, it's true that they wallow in mud but they do that to keep cool as their pink skin (not that dissimilar to ours) gets easily sunburned. Wallowing also serves to clean their skin of any pests or parasites. Unlike most creatures, they never wee or poo in their beds. And, as I've mentioned before, given the opportunity to shower with clean water, a pig will usually do just that.

Milk snakes lay their eggs – about a dozen of them at a time – in piles of animal manure.

Of all the creatures on the planet, the New Zealand sea lion (also known as Hooker's sea lion) would probably win a foul breath competition. It's breath is said to be truly disgusting. Mind you, whales aren't much better. In fact, they have such terrible breath, sailors used to believe that just a single whiff of it could cause brain disorders.

ENGROSSING
SCIENCE

In the 1970s, scientists successfully transplanted a monkey's head onto another monkey's body.

Staying with monkeys . . . for an experiment in maternal attachment (how mammals interact with their mothers), scientists raised three groups of monkeys. Some were raised by their mother. Some were raised by a stationary Chlorox bottle covered with fur. The last group were raised by a Chlorox bottle also covered with fur that was remotely controlled and acted rather like a real mother. The monkeys with the furry moving bottle mother grew up nearly as normal as those raised with a real mother, but those with the stationary mother gradually became mad and distressed.

Ever wondered how they produce antidotes to snake venom (poison)? Snake handlers, working with scientists, goad the snakes into lashing out and parting with their venom. This venom is then used to make an antidote to help save people who are later bitten by snakes from that species.

In the new science of zoopharmacognosy, scientists patiently watch animals to learn about how they medicate themselves – in other words, make themselves better. The word zoopharmacognosy – derived from the words zoo (animal), pharma (drug), and gnosy (knowing) – was invented by an American professor named Eloy Rodriguez. He observed apes selecting a particular part of a medicinal plant by removing the leaves, then breaking the stem to suck out the juice. According to Dr Rodriguez, 'Some of the compounds we've identified by zoopharmacognosy kill parasitic worms, and some of these chemicals may be useful against tumours (cancer). There is no question that the templates for most drugs are in the natural world.'

Wouldn't it be amazing if we could learn from animals how to cure cancer?

ENGROSSING BODY PARTS

The glass frog has a transparent stomach, so you can see its intestines and all its innards . . . URGH!

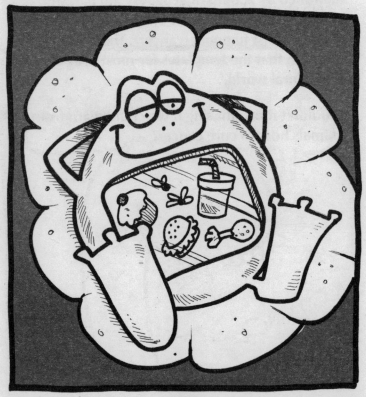

If unfolded and laid out flat, the membranes in a dog's nose would be larger than the dog itself.

Frogs have eardrums on the outside of their bodies – behind their eyes.

The giant plant-eating dinosaur *Brachiosaurus* had nostrils on the top of its head. It also had teeth shaped like chisels (and a very small brain).

Dogs have a very powerful sense of hearing. This explains why they are reluctant to go out in the rain. It's not just that they don't like getting wet: the rain amplifies sound and actually hurts the dog's ears.

A mouse's tail is as long as its body. It's also scaly to help the mouse grip when climbing.

A mouse's incisors (front teeth) never stop growing. They're ground down by all the gnawing it does. If it weren't for that, their incisors could grow up to 13 centimetres long in a year.

Large whales have a blowhole crest. This is an elevated area in front of their blowholes that stops water getting in while they're breathing. Makes sense when you think about it.

An anteater's claws are vital for its survival as it needs them to dig into ants' nests to find food, so it protects them by walking on its knuckles – which makes it look as if it's limping.

Great white sharks have large dagger-like teeth.

A starfish can regrow an arm if one is torn off –

all the more remarkable when you consider that they don't have brains. A career in reality TV shows beckons!

Squid have three hearts.

Fish that live more than half a mile below the surface of the ocean don't have eyes.

The giant anteater has a strange connected nose and mouth and no teeth! Its nose looks like a tapered cylinder and it's rigid, not fleshy. Within this huge snout is a massive half-metre-long sticky tongue, used for scooping ants and termites from their hiding places. You'd think that the snout would inhale a lot of dirt while it's eating, but the anteater has the extraordinary ability to seal off its nose.

Another creature which can seal off its nostrils – this time from sandstorm debris – is the Bactrian camel, which lives in the deserts of Mongolia and China, an inhospitable, arid environment. To help it survive these dry conditions, the camel's lungs and nose can work together to trap any moisture in the desert air.

The leg bones of a bat are so thin that no bat can walk on them.

The catfish has over 27,000 taste buds – more than any other creature.

The heart of a blue whale is the size of a small car.

Sea otters have the densest fur of any creature –
100,000 hairs per square centimetre. That's about
the same in a square centimetre as humans have
on their entire head.

The giant squid is the largest creature without a backbone. It weighs up to 2.5 metric tons and grows up to 16 metres long. Each eye is almost half a metre in diameter.

Penguins have an organ above their eyes that converts seawater to fresh water.

Lemon sharks grow a new set of teeth every two weeks. They grow more than 24,000 new teeth every year.

A shark's stomach has the capacity to stretch so that the shark can consume large amounts of food quickly. Similarly, having an elastic stomach allows the deep-sea anglerfish to swallow prey larger than itself.

An ostrich's eye is the size of a tennis ball, and bigger than its brain. This isn't its only peculiarity: unlike most birds, which have three or four toes, the ostrich has just two.

Minnows (small fish) have teeth in their throats.

An alligator can go through 2,000 – 3,000 teeth in a lifetime.

The babirusa, or pig-deer, of the Indonesian islands has tusks formed by their greatly elongated canine teeth. Two of these amazing teeth pierce its flesh and grow through the top of its muzzle to become tusks.

A hippo can open its mouth wide enough to fit a child inside.

Lizards and snakes shed their skin. In the case of snakes, it normally comes off in a single layer, taking with it any parasites that have attached themselves to it. Snakes do this three or four times a year.

Lizards, on the other hand, shed their skin in patches, with small pieces coming off at different times. Different lizards have different intervals between periods of shedding, but when it comes to shedding-time, all lizards' skin becomes dull, and small white patches appear over their bodies. The actual act of shedding is achieved by rubbing their bodies against things found in their habitat, with the top layer of old skin coming off in pieces. They will also tear bits of skin off with their mouths, and sometimes eat the skin. Doing this sounds gross but is actually healthy as the old skin contains important vitamins.

The Ozark blind salamander has eyes when it is born. So how does it get its name? Well, as it matures, its eyes shrink and its eyelids fuse together, making it blind. But as it mainly lives in caves in pitch darkness, it doesn't need to see.

ENGROSSING SURVIVAL

Some alligators can survive the winter by allowing their heads to be completely frozen – just leaving their nose out to breathe for months on end.

Ever wondered why a dog puts its tail between its legs? It's actually an important survival tool. Dogs' bottoms carry personal scents that identify them. When dogs put their tails between their legs they're covering the smell. Think of it like frightened people putting up their hands to hide their face.

A threatened horn lizard can shoot blood from its eyes for over a metre. It's a useful survival trick that serves to surprise would-be predators and enables the lizard to escape.

Most marine fish could survive in a tank filled with human blood.

Sharks will eat anything – but not in the vicinity of where they give birth. This is the only way nature stops them from accidentally eating their own babies.

Only one in a 1,000 creatures born in the sea survives to maturity.

To survive, many birds must eat half their own weight in food each day.

When a pair of rhinos feels threatened, they

stand back to back, confronting their enemies from opposite directions.

To escape predators, the flying fish builds up speed in the water then leaps into the air. Once in the air, it can stay airborne for up to 100 metres.

Ostriches use their powerful legs as a means of defence. They can kick a lion to death.

Some snakes can survive for up to a year without eating.

Even though cuttlefish are colour-blind they can change colour to camouflage themselves.

If captured, a bullfrog pretends to be dead but then quickly hops away if its captor releases its grip.

The sea cucumber, a relative of the starfish, has the incredible ability to change parts of its body from solid to liquid in order to escape predators – for instance allowing it to squeeze through a tiny hole, before turning solid again.

Octopus and squid can change their skin colour. Normally brown, their skin becomes green or blue when they are under threat.

The orang-utan's warning signal to would-be aggressors is a loud belch.

A hippo's main enemies are crocodiles, lions and hyenas. To survive, the hippo has developed an extraordinary technique. It turns its bottom to its enemy and lets fly with a shower of poo! Yup, that'll show 'em.

A flock of starlings flies in loose formation – until a bird of prey appears. Then the flock tightens up so the predator doesn't have a single bird to strike at.

The mudfish can survive in mud for a year until the rain comes.

The aardvark – everyone's favourite beginning-of-the-dictionary animal – depends on its acute senses and digging abilities for survival. It's so sensitive, even a moderate blow to its head can kill it.

The West Indian wood snake has a clever trick when confronted by a predator: it pretends to be dead. It lies very still and allows its eyes to fill up with blood and turn red. The blood then drips out of the snake's mouth, which makes it look as if it's completely deceased. Fortunately for this particular snake, its main predators will only eat food that they themselves have killed.

There's a frog in South America that has a fabulous survival tool. Whenever a predator comes along, the frog turns its back and 'moons' at it! No, honestly. The frog's bottom has (what looks like) two enormous eyes that make it seem as if it's much bigger than it really is – frightening off the would-be attacker! If that doesn't work, the frog can also let rip with a foul-smelling liquid. Now those are what I call superpowers!

When being chased by predators, lizards have the ability to shed their tails. This might sound a little drastic, but lizards shed skin and, besides, what use is a tail if you're dead? Far better to let a predator have the tail than the rest of your body – rather like us shedding a coat when grabbed by a would-be robber!

Bobcats take to the water when they're being chased (e.g. by dogs) because they can swim so much better than their pursuers. But a bobcat's survival abilities don't end there: its spotty coat camouflages it in the rocks it calls home – in much the same way the similar-shaped plain lynx merges with the forest.

Skunks use their unpleasant odour to keep would-be predators away. The smell is so powerful that it can be detected a mile away. A skunk has two glands just behind its tail that are responsible for the foul-smelling spray. Think of them as bum nozzles, which the skunk can wield like spray-guns or water-pistols that can fire up to three metres. Except that they're not spraying water but the vilest liquid imaginable that can cause temporary blindness and vomiting. At least the spotted skunk gives a warning by doing a handstand before spraying. Bet it still doesn't give you time to get a whole mile clear!

Let's not just think about other creatures' survival: let's consider our own! As previous readers will know, if you are chased by a crocodile, run from side to side – a crocodile isn't good at making sharp turns. However, if it catches you, push your thumbs into its eyeballs – it will open its jaws and let you go at once.

OH, THAT'S TOO GROSS!

The frigate bird chases birds until they throw up and then – really gross fact alert! – eats their puke.

One of the remedies recommended to ward off or cure the Black Death – bubonic plague in medieval times – was to put the intestines of young pigeons or puppies on the forehead. Another neat trick was to sit in a sewer while shaving a live chicken's bottom and then strapping it to your armpit. Like you do.

In 2004, while snorkelling in Australia, Luke Tresoglavic was bitten by a small wobbegong carpet shark that refused to let go. Poor Luke had to swim to the shore and then drive to get help . . . with the shark still attached to his leg! Can you think of anything worse, because I'm not sure that I can?

Egyptian dentists used to suggest putting half a freshly killed, hot mouse in your mouth to cure bad breath. Obviously it would do a lot to cause – rather than to cure – bad breath, but it does have this to say for it: if you put a freshly killed, hot mouse in your mouth every day, then sure as eggs is eggs, nothing worse than that is going to happen to you that day.

There are animals – such as lions and chimpanzees – that kill young members of their own species just so that they can persuade their poor victims' mothers to have 'new' babies with them. What a truly wicked thing to do!

Some fungal spores spread by growing on mouse droppings. When other mice come along and smell the droppings, the spores stick to the whiskers of the mice and that's how they spread.

During heavy snowfalls, turkeys get snow stuck in their air passages and suffocate.

In Ireland, geese were once used to sweep chimneys. They would be pulled up chimneys by a rope tied to their legs and then the beating of their wings would dislodge the soot.

Tiger snakes can survive perfectly well after their eyes have been pecked out by seagulls.

In the Middle Ages, cat poo was used by women to prevent facial hair growth. What made it worse was that it almost certainly didn't work. And why did they do it? 'Because I'm worth it.'

Eagles like to eat tortoises and turtles. They fly

around with their prey until they see a suitable rock or stone. Then they drop the tortoise or turtle on it and, if all goes according to plan, the shell cracks and the eagle gets to eat the contents. According to legend, the ancient Greek playwright, Aeschylus, was killed when an eagle dropped a tortoise on his head. The eagle had mistaken the playwright's bald head for a rock. Doh!

A sea squirt found in the seas around Japan eats its own brain. When it reaches maturity, it attaches itself to a rock and, with no further need to move, dispenses with its brain by digesting it.

Mitchell Symons
HOW MUCH POO DOES AN ELEPHANT DO?*

... and further fascinating facts!

* An elephant produces an eye-wateringly pongy 20 kilograms of dung a day!

Let Mitchell Symons be your guide into the weird and wonderful world of trivia.

- Camels are born without humps
- Walt Disney, creator of Mickey Mouse, was scared of mice
- Only 30% of humans can flare their nostrils
- A group of twelve or more cows is called a flink

Mitchell Symons
WHY DO FARTS SMELL LIKE ROTTEN EGGS?

... and more crazy facts
explained!

Ever wondered ...

- Why we burp?
- What a wotsit is?
- Whether lemmings really jump off cliffs?
- Why vomit always contains carrots?
- And why *do* farts smell like rotten eggs?

No subject is too strange and no trivia
too tough for Mitchell Symons, who has
the answers to these crazy questions, and
many more.

Q: Who writes the best books on farts, bogeys and other yucky stuff?

A: Mitchell Symons, of course

Q: What's his website called?

A: Grossbooks.co.uk, what else!

On this site you can:
- Win cool stuff in quizzes and competitions
- Add your own fab facts and publish them online
- Be first to find out about Mitchell's new books before they're published

As Mitchell's mum would say:
'Thank goodness it's not *scratch 'n' sniff...* '

See for yourself at **Grossbooks.co.uk**